Tea at Glenbrooke

A Quiet Place Where Souls Are Refreshed

Robin Jones Gunn *with paintings by* Susan Mink Colclough

BLUE COTTAGE GIFTS™
a division of Multnomah Publishers, Inc.®
Sisters, Oregon

Tea at Glenbrooke
©2001 by Robin Jones Gunn
Published by Blue Cottage Gifts™, a division of Multnomah Publishers, Inc.®
P.O. Box 1720, Sisters, Oregon 97759

ISBN 1-58860-023-8

The Glenbrooke Series
by Robin Jones Gunn

*Secrets, Whispers, Echoes, Sunsets, Clouds,
Waterfalls, Woodlands, Wildflowers*

Visit Robin's Web site at www.robingunn.com

Artwork © Arts Uniq'®, Inc.
Artwork designs by Susan Mink Colclough are reproduced under license from Arts Uniq'®, Inc., Cookeville, Tennessee, and may not be reproduced without permission. For information regarding art prints featured in this book, please contact:

> *Arts Uniq'®, Inc.*
> *P.O. Box 3085*
> *Cookeville, Tennessee 38502*
> *1-800-223-5020*

Designed by Koechel Peterson & Associates, Minneapolis, Minnesota

Multnomah Publishers, Inc., has made every effort to trace the ownership of all poems and quotes. In the event of a question arising from the use of a poem or quote, we regret any error made and will be pleased to make the necessary correction in future editions of this book.

Scripture quotations are taken from *The Holy Bible,* New King James Version ©1984 by Thomas Nelson, Inc.; *The Living Bible* (TLB) ©1971, used by permission of Tyndale House Publishers, Inc.; *The Holy Bible,* New International Version (NIV) ©1973, 1984 by International Bible Society, used by permission of Zondervan Publishing House.

Printed in China

01 02 03 04 05 06—10 9 8 7 6 5 4 3 2 1 0

www.bluecottagegifts.com

A special thank you to Cyndie May for research and recipe testing

Dedication

To the readers of the Glenbrooke novels...especially to
those who have written charming letters to me over the
years. Each of you has opened your heart yet never asked
me to return the kindness. I do so now on these pages.

And to the most precious women in my life:
my grandma, Great Lady;
my mom, Barbara;
my sister, Julie;
my daughter, Rachel;
and my best friend, Donna.
For always.

Contents

Welcome!

When was the last time you took a long, leisurely bubble bath or spent a summer afternoon in the hammock? Can you remember the last time you lingered by a cheery fireplace while the winter winds raged outside? That's the kind of moment offered to you when you come for tea at Glenbrooke.

My sister, Julie, and I had a playhouse in our backyard when we were growing up. We often would escape to our own little world in that playhouse. Mom made sure our box of dress-up clothes included silly, frilly hats and long strings of beads.

Whenever we grew tired of playing school, we would play tea party. Our tea was poured from a red plastic teapot that had been filled with water from the garden hose. Our cookies usually were the invisible kind but nonetheless scrumptious.

On the rare occasions when the cookies were real, our little brother, Kevin, would invariably show up at the Dutch door, begging an invitation to join us. We almost always shooed him away and put out the "No Boys Allowed" sign.

I have no recollection of what Julie and I talked about at our tea parties or how we instinctively knew that was a time set apart just for us girls. But I learned in those early years a truth that I still believe with all my heart: Whenever women (of any age) come together over tea, something rich and nurturing happens. When heads are bent close and hearts are opened wide, an outpouring of friendship, serenity, beauty, comfort, grace, joy, hope, and peace occurs. A whole cupful!

The day my youngest started kindergarten, Julie met me at the elementary school and took me to a quaint teashop that had mismatched pottery and different patterned tablecloths on each table. We sipped herbal blends of flower-laced teas, and she consoled me as only an older sister can.

When my friend Anne journeyed from the Netherlands all the way to my corner of the world, I set up a tea party in the backyard and invited a special group of one-hearted friends. Our laughter filled the air and lingered in all our lives for weeks.

Just two nights ago, my longtime friend, Rahnella, came and sat by my fire. I filled a favorite teapot with my precious, limited supply of Lady Grey tea from Ireland and lit a candle.

"Read me one of your stories," Rahnella said, as she put up her feet and wrapped her hands around the smooth china cup. In the twilight that lit the room, I read to her.

An hour later the tea was gone. The rest of the family had returned, bringing with them the sounds of doors closing, the refrigerator opening, and the dog barking.

Rahnella's husband stepped into our mellow, candlelit haven and said, "You two sure look relaxed."

"That's because we just shared a Glenbrooke moment," Rahnella told him.

"Is that one of those chick-things you like to do with a pot of tea and those little sugar cubes?" he asked.

Rahnella ignored his comment and asked me, "Do you still have that 'No Boys Allowed' sign?"

We laughed and gave each other a knowing nod. Only a woman understands what an hour with Lady Grey by candlelight can do for one's soul.

With that in mind, it is my pleasure to invite you to tea at Glenbrooke. Come, please. Make yourself comfy and join in a celebration of gentle moments in this quiet place where souls are refreshed. I've kept the teapot under the cozy and a china cup waiting just for you.

Kettle's on, cups are waiting,
Favorite chairs anticipating,
No matter what I have to do,
My friend, there's always time for you.

D. MORGAN

Tea of Friendship

Friendship? Yes, please!

CHARLES DICKENS

Lilacs in May

My treasures are my friends.

Constantine

The air is thick with the scent of lilacs. Never have I seen such a riotous explosion as festoons this lilac bush! I pause before climbing the three steps up to the porch where Carrie waits for me. My lungs can barely hold the sweetness of the heady fragrance.

Carrie smiles. I lower myself into the welcoming white wicker rocker beside her. The hundred-year-old boards beneath us complain as we begin to rock.

At first we don't talk. We just sit. And rock. Inhaling the air laced with purple lilacs.

On the low table between us a tall pitcher of iced tea awaits. The warmth of the May afternoon causes the ice cubes to shuffle lazily, bumping the sides of the glass pitcher. The cubes sound like a submerged wind chime.

I know I should say something. But I have forgotten for the moment what it was that prompted me to call Carrie and invite myself into the middle of her afternoon.

She doesn't seem to mind my silence. Her gaze is fixed on the large, fuzzy bees at work in the lilac bush. The funny fellows appear to be carrying as much pollen as any diligent bee could be expected to bear. Yet they don't fly home. They pull themselves out of the lush flowers, hover unsteadily, and then, finding they are enchanted beyond their ability to break the fragrant spell, they dive in for more golden pollen. More, more, until they barely can fly. Off goes the smaller one. His companion takes notice and follows in the flight of the loopy bumblebees. It is the giddy dance of May.

Carrie and I make silly comments about the drunken bees. She pours the iced tea, and we visit for an hour or so. We speak of nothing and everything. The bees have returned for more lilac dust, and we watch them as we talk and nod and chuckle together.

I wonder, is this the way good friends lightly step through the giddy dance of May? Meeting on the front porch. Sharing the moment. Knowing each other by heart. Dancing our own dance, exchanging fragrance for music.

And there is music. The ice's muffled clinking, the bees' low hum, the wicker chairs' steady rocking on the creaking boards.

This is what I came for. This giddy dance. This fragrance. This music that has no words. This front row seat at the afternoon matinee of "Loopy Bees in the Lilac Bush."

Now I can return to the tasks I had left undone at home. My heart is light. God is in his heaven. All is right with the world.

I don't need to explain any of this to Carrie. True friends understand what it means to meet on the front porch. It is, after all, the safest place for a woman to be while under the influence of lilacs in May.

On May Morning

Hail, bounteous May! That does inspire
Mirth, and youth, and warm desire;
Woods and groves are of thy dressing;
Hill and dale doth boast thy blessing.

Thus we salute thee with our early song,
And welcome thee, and wish thee long.

JOHN MILTON

11

~Front Porch Tea Menu~

Iced Mint Tea
Mom's Chicken Salad Sandwiches
Citrus Tea Bread

Mom's Chicken Salad Sandwiches

Makes: 6 servings

2 cups chopped, boiled chicken breast

1½ cups finely chopped celery

¾ cup mayonnaise

¼ teaspoon sweet pickle relish

½ cup chopped red seedless grapes

12 slices crusty French or Italian bread

Combine the first five ingredients in a bowl, cover and refrigerate at least 2 hours so that the flavor will develop.

Slice loaf of crusty bread on the diagonal about ½ inch thick. Just before serving spread a small amount of chicken salad evenly on the bread. Garnish with sliced grapes or celery leaves.

Citrus Tea Bread

Makes: 1 loaf

Bread:

1 large grapefruit	¼ teaspoon salt
¾ cup sugar	2 tablespoons butter at room temperature
2 cups flour	1 egg
¾ teaspoon baking soda	1 teaspoon vanilla extract
⅛ teaspoon dried lemon zest	½ cup chopped pecans or other nuts
½ teaspoon baking powder	

Glaze:

¼ cup confectioners' sugar	¼ teaspoon lemon extract
1 tablespoon water	

Preheat oven to 350°. Spray an 8½ x 4½ inch loaf pan with nonstick cooking spray. Set aside.

Grate the rind of the grapefruit until you have 1 teaspoon of zest and set aside. Peel and section grapefruit over your work bowl so as to catch all the juices. Remove the membranes from the outside of the grapefruit sections. Squeeze the grapefruit sections to release all the juices. Discard grapefruit membranes. In a food processor place grapefruit sections and juice. Blend 15 seconds until the grapefruit sections have somewhat broken up. Measure 1¼ cups of the grapefruit mixture. Any remaining mixture may be frozen for later use.

Combine grapefruit rind, sugar, flour, baking soda, lemon zest, baking powder, and salt. Blend together well.

Combine the 1¼ cups grapefruit mixture, butter, egg and vanilla; stir well. Add the dry ingredients and stir until moist. Fold in the chopped pecans.

Pour batter into prepared loaf pan. Bake for one hour or until a toothpick inserted into the center will be clean when removed. Remove from oven. Place on wire rack while in pan.

Prepare the glaze by combining the confectioners' sugar, lemon extract, and water in a small bowl. Stir until completely dissolved. Drizzle glaze over bread while still in the pan. Let the bread cool 10 minutes before removing. Place bread on wire rack and cool completely.

Sunset Tea
A Cup

OF SERENITY

Wild Are the Waves

Wild are the waves when the wind blows;
But fishes in the deep
Live in a world of waters,
Still as sleep.

Wild are the skies when Winter
Roars at the doors of Spring;
But when his lamentation's lulled
Then sweet birds sing.

WALTER DE LA MARE

When Day Is Done

Streamers of pink satin ribbons flutter across the primrose sky. The sun, looking like a great, orange and yellow-frosted sugar cookie, is about to be dunked into the ocean's wide-rimmed cup.

The day is done.

And here we sit, nestled in pockets of tawny sand, pockets that still hold the warmth of the fleeting day. The ever-dancing breezes make their farewell, brushing kisses across our cheeks as off they go. Somewhere, across the sapphire sea, they will greet a new day as it opens its eyes.

But here, the day is done.

My husband lights a match, and the gathered kindling sparks. Slowly the flames rise like slender arms, eager to embrace the driftwood. A settled hush comes over the beach, as twilight draws close this circle of friends.

My teenage daughter sits perfectly still, her back straight, gazing into the dancing flames. She's careful not to move as a friend folds my daughter's hair into a long braid.

In the south corner of the sky a full moon rises. Another perfectly round sugar cookie. Only this one comes unfrosted, fresh from heaven's oven. This soft, vanilla moon glides effortlessly across the night sky.

Little Anna cuddles up next to me. I take the sleepy toddler onto my lap where she settles in with a contented sigh. The scent of the sun's caresses rises from her golden hair, filling me with memories of when my own children were this small. On her feet she has donned booties of caramel-colored sand, knit in place grain by grain with dried salt water. Her lips pucker into the shape of a tender, pink heart.

In the gentle rhythm of Anna's unlabored breathing resides no fear. No worry. No anxiety over tomorrow's troubles.

The day is done.

I close my eyes and remember that I, too, am held fast in everlasting arms. This day is done. I am not a twirling wind, sent to chase the sun into the blazing tomorrow. I must rest.

As Anna sleeps in my arms, my heart catches a ride on the silent, ivory moon, and for the first time in many weeks, I am immersed in serenity.

Taps

Day is done, gone the sun,
From the hills, from the lake,
From the skies.
All is well, safely rest,
God is nigh.

Thanks and praise, for our days,
'Neath the sun, 'neath the stars,
'Neath the sky,
As we go, this we know,
God is nigh.

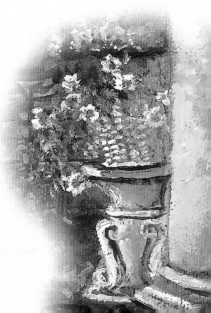

~Sunset Tea Menu~

Iced Tea with Lemon Slices
More S'mores, Please!
Red Grapes
Biscuits over the Coals

More S'mores, Please!

Makes: 8 servings

1 package honey graham crackers

1 large or several small plain chocolate bars

1 bag large marshmallows

1 roasting stick or long-handled cooking fork

Place 1 marshmallow securely on the end of the roasting stick or cooking fork. Hold over the campfire until the marshmallow is cooked to your desired color.

Remove 1 large graham cracker or 2 half crackers from package.

Place the roasted marshmallow on one half of the graham cracker.

Place a piece of chocolate on the other side of the graham cracker. Close the two halves together as if to make a sandwich.

Biscuits over the Coals

Makes: 9 servings

2 ¼ cups all-purpose baking mix

⅔ cup milk

2–3 tablespoons sugar

3 tablespoons butter

Foil

Mix all the ingredients together.

Place a small fistful of dough onto a piece of foil. Carefully close up the foil to leave an air space above the dough so as not to squish it.

Place the foil on the warm coals of the campfire. Take care not to place the foil on the flame or it will burn the biscuit.

Check biscuit in 15–20 minutes for doneness. The biscuit will be done when a knife inserted into it comes out clean. Depending on the fire coals it may take 30–40 minutes to cook the biscuits.

To serve, simply split the biscuit in half and top with either Sweet Butter or Peach Garnish.

Sweet Butter

Makes: ½ cup

4 tablespoons softened butter

¼ cup honey

Combine ingredients and blend well. Chill for 2 hours before serving. Place an ample amount on a split biscuit.

Peach Garnish

Makes: 4 servings

Canned sliced peaches, drained

Brown sugar

Place sliced peaches on half of the open campfire biscuit. Sprinkle the peaches with a little brown sugar.

Tea
OF BEAUTY

Earth's crammed
with heaven,
And every common bush
afire with God.

Only he who sees
takes off his shoes,
The rest
sit around and pluck blackberries.

ELIZABETH BARRETT BROWNING

Where Wildflowers Grew

Listen! The wind is rising, and the air is wild with leaves.
We have had our summer evenings, now for October eves!

Haambert Wolfe

The wildflowers are all gone. The Queen Anne's lace has disappeared. So have the blue cornflowers and the dainty, yellow buttercups.

All summer the field by the mailbox was full of them. The entire knoll wore the wildflowers like a brightly embroidered shawl. Every time I walked down to the mailbox under the warm August skies, I smiled at the flowers, and they waved back. Every day.

Today, they're all gone. Done. Dried and blown on the wind. The knoll has exchanged the laughing colors of summer for the golden mantle of approaching fall. Deeper, more thoughtful amber shades now stretch across the countryside.

Next Tuesday the jolly, yellow school bus will roll down this street. It will open its smiling mouth and swallow my youngest in one bite. I will stand right here and watch as she joins the other scrubbed faces at the windows. I will wave at them, and they will smile back at me. Every day.

A new season is starting. A beautiful new season. A season with brisk mornings, fat pumpkins, and translucent, yellow maple leaves.

But no wildflowers.

I will miss the afternoon melody of the ice cream truck. In its place will come the afternoon whistling of my teakettle and steaming cups of Irish Breakfast tea with a splash of cream and a dash of sugar. The fragrance of pool chlorine permeating my daughter's skin will be exchanged for the scent of freshly sharpened wood from a #2 pencil. Instead of slicing into a round watermelon and lighting the barbecue, we'll soon be dining on slow-cooked stew and whole grain rolls still warm from the oven. I will light candles in my living room when the sun goes down, and the air will fill with the scent of cinnamon laced with vanilla.

One season of beauty is about to be exchanged for another. Each is beautiful and wonderful in its own way. I need to remember this. I need to cling to the truth that "He has made everything beautiful in its season" and "there is a time for every purpose under heaven."

I must believe this is true because, you see, yesterday our son left for college. The end of one season, the beginning of another.

As we drove away from the dorm, I felt a force greater than my own muscles tightening around my abdomen. "Oh, my stomach," I moaned.

"Are you okay?" my husband asked.

"Are you sick, Mom?" My daughter looked worried.

"No, I'm not sick."

"What does it feel like?" she asked.

"It feels like…it feels like contractions."

She looked at me oddly. "Aren't those what you get when your baby is about to come?"

I nodded. Then I told my daughter a great secret of womanhood that I didn't know until that very moment. "I guess you also get contractions when your baby is about to leave."

I didn't cry. I'm not crying today.

I know it's the next season in his life. I'm happy for him. Delighted that he's moving on in such a wonderful direction. The transition is natural and beautiful. Really.

Yet here I stand, in the middle of the road beside the mailbox, staring at where the wildflowers grew. I can't move. I can barely breathe as another contraction washes over me.

Yesterday my boy was here, running down this laughing knoll, his hair the color of buttercups, his eyes as blue as cornflowers.

Today, all the wildflowers are gone. And so is he.

But I'm confident that one of these brisk, autumn weekends, when the house smells of meatloaf and baked potatoes, the front door will open and there will stand my wildflower boy. He'll be a little taller, a little wiser. Over his shoulder will be slung a duffel bag stuffed with dirty clothes.

And all my contractions will mysteriously disappear.

A thing of beauty is a joy forever;
Its loveliness increases;
It will never
Pass into nothingness.

JOHN KEATS

Now Autumn Comes

Now autumn comes, the air grows strangely pale,
To fall the reddened apple needs no gale,
The storks have long since left the yellowing land,
The night grows cold, and All-Saints is at hand.
The leaves will soon be shed, now heart finds heart.
—Dear, is it time for you and me to part?

CARL BUSSE
TRANSLATED BY JETHRO BITHELL

The golden eve is all astir,
And tides of sunset flood on us
Incredible, miraculous
We look with adoration on
Beauty coming, beauty gone,
That waits not any looking on.

JAMES STEPHENS

~Wildflower Tea Menu~

Irish Breakfast Tea
Pumpkin Streusel Muffins
Sliced Apple

Pumpkin Streusel Muffins

Makes: 6 servings

⅓ cup whole wheat flour

⅓ cup flour

⅓ cup sugar

3 tablespoons wheat germ

¼ cup + 2 tablespoons raisins

1 ½ teaspoons baking powder

½ teaspoon salt

½ teaspoon baking soda

1 cup pumpkin puree

1 egg

1 teaspoon pumpkin pie spice

½ teaspoon vanilla extract

¼ cup orange juice

2 tablespoons chopped walnuts

Streusel Topping

⅛ cup quick oats

1/16 teaspoon pumpkin pie spice

½ tablespoon butter

½ tablespoon brown sugar

Preheat oven to 350°. Grease and flour muffin tin.

In a large bowl combine the flours, sugar, wheat germ, raisins, baking powder, salt, and baking soda. In another bowl blend together pumpkin puree, egg, pumpkin pie spice, vanilla, and orange juice.

Add the pumpkin mixture to the dry ingredients and mix until combined.

Fill the 6 muffin cups ⅔ full. Top with walnuts.

Blend together all ingredients for the streusel topping using a fork.

Sprinkle the topping on the walnuts. Bake 25-30 minutes or until a knife inserted comes out clean.

OF GRACE

She Walks in Beauty

She walks in beauty, like the night
Of cloudless climes and starry skies;
And all that's best of dark and bright
Meet in her aspect and her eyes....
And on that cheek, and o'er that brow,
So soft, so calm, yet eloquent,
The smiles that win, the tints that glow,
But tell of days in goodness spent,
A mind at peace with all below,
A heart whose love is innocent!

LORD BYRON

In Praise of Afternoon Tea Time

There are few hours in life more agreeable than the hour dedicated to the ceremony known as afternoon tea.

HENRY JAMES, PORTRAIT OF A LADY

We have a woman to thank for the introduction of the elegant, British-style afternoon tea.

Anna, the Duchess of Bedford (1788–1861), lived her life in aristocratic homes where two daily mealtimes were strictly observed. The first meal was served around noon and consisted of bread and beef. Dinner was a huge meal but never served until at least six in the evening and more commonly at eight.

As a middle-aged woman, Anna apparently lost patience with this dining schedule. To remedy the "peckish, sinking feeling" she experienced while waiting for dinner, Anna requested one summer afternoon that a tray of tea and buttered bread be sent up to her rooms at Belvoir Castle. This was unusual, but, since a duchess has the right to make such requests, her servants quickly obliged her.

Anna enjoyed the experience so much she invited friends to join her each afternoon. The menu grew to include small cakes, bread and butter sandwiches, assorted sweets, and, of course, tea.

When the Duchess returned to London in the fall, she sent cards to her friends asking them to join her in the afternoon for "tea and a walking the fields." During the mid-1800s, London still contained large, open meadows within the city.

Other hostesses, who were delighted with a new opportunity to socialize, soon picked up the lovely pastime. Special gowns were designed for teatime. Tea sets and all the necessary accoutrements were in demand. Scones were added to the afternoon fare as well as "biscuits" or cookies and whatever else the hostess might serve to impress her guests.

A common pattern of service soon merged. The chairs were drawn close. The tea table was set with fine porcelain from China and with a variety of tea "dainties." The first pot of tea was made in the kitchen and carried to the lady of the house who waited with her invited guests. The hostess warmed the awaiting pot from a second pot (usually silver) that was kept heated over a small flame. Food and tea were then passed among the guests. Graceful posture and good manners were expected as the guests joined in quiet conversation.

Thus the "civilized" afternoon teatime was born and has remained, with all its elegant implications.

There is a great deal of poetry and fine sentiment in a chest of tea.

RALPH WALDO EMERSON,
LETTERS AND SOCIAL AIMS

An RSVP to Grace

She will set a garland of grace on your head
and present you with a crown of splendor.

PROVERBS 4:9 NIV

A swirl of autumn leaves crunched beneath my nicest pair of shoes. I trotted as fast as I could up the steps of the Victorian Tea House. Janet's invitation stated that our reservation was for the four o'clock seating. In my RSVP I had promised to meet her in the lobby.

And I was late.

Only a few minutes, but not a good way to start our business relationship. First impressions and all that. The problem was I had changed outfits three times and still wasn't convinced I was wearing the right ensemble for a formal afternoon tea.

Janet was waiting for me beside the ornate fountain just inside the door. She smiled when she saw me and politely shook my hand. The maître d' showed us into the parlor and pulled out the chairs at our reserved corner table. I glanced to the left, then to the right, then down, then across the table at Janet. Ours were the only bare hands in this opulent tearoom. The women around us all wore gloves! Gloves and hats and stunning afternoon suits. My idea of an appropriate frock for this high tea was all wrong.

Tall palms bent over me, as if clucking their tongues in a quiet mocking of my lack of chic. Thick Persian rugs silenced the waiter's steps, as he delivered a tiered tray of fancy sweets and tall, silver pots of Earl Grey tea. I felt like a country mouse, quite willing to make a speedy escape from this world in which I did not fit.

Not Janet.

She smiled demurely at the waiter, thanking him as he poured Earl into her china cup. With her shoulders straight and head high, Janet entered into the moment without exhibiting the slightest hint of intimidation. She was a gloveless wonder.

The soothing strains of harp music floated above our bare heads. I watched Janet take tiny nibbles of her petit four and gracefully lift her cloth napkin to tap away a speck of almond-flavored icing. She bent close and listened to me as if everything I had to say was fascinating.

Janet stirred her tea slowly. She knew how to appropriately squeeze the slice of lemon that came to the table wearing a tiny lace shower cap.

The longer we sat there, the more comfortable I became. I found I could sit a little straighter. My voice could lower. I could tilt my head just so and listen with a pleasant expression the way Janet listened to me. It didn't matter what anyone else around us was wearing or how others were conducting their afternoon ritual. This was our teatime. We could make it whatever we wanted it to be.

And Janet was making it a lovely event. She didn't compare either of us to anyone else inside the rounded corners of that gardenia-scented room. Not a pinch of gossip or haughtiness seasoned her conversation. By her facial expression and her clear gaze, I knew she had thrown wide the front gate of her heart. "Come in," her demeanor beckoned to me. "Come, just as you are. I welcome you without hesitation."

She made me feel as if it didn't matter that I'd been late or that I was underdressed or that, in my inexperience with tea fare, I expressed surprise at finding a slice of cucumber inside my tiny sandwich. I was welcomed into her life.

That's when Janet taught me the first lesson in the elegance of friendship: Grace invites grace.

In the fifteen years since that memorable autumn afternoon, Janet and I have taken tea at a dozen locations, some elegant, some homey. Yet it never matters where we are or what is going on around us. It's our time. Our ritual. Our friendship growing in grace. Every time we meet, I sit a little straighter, talk a little softer, listen a little more attentively.

Hearts inclined toward each other. Grace inviting grace. Elegant, stately, steadfast grace.

Such grace always receives a "Yes, please!" RSVP to its invitation.

~Elegant Tea Menu~

Your Favorite Regular Loose Tea
Celebration Punch
Orange Scones with Citrus Butter
Turkey Salad and Cranberry Relish Pastry Cups
Crab Triangles
Stuffed Cherry Tomatoes
Pears with Chantilly Dressing
Pineapple Dessert
Almond Tea Cake
Butter Mints
Mixed Nuts
Strawberries and Cream

Celebration Punch

Makes: 8 servings

1 cup water

2 cups cranberry juice

¼ cup sugar

½ cup pineapple juice

3 cinnamon sticks

1 teaspoon whole cloves

1 quart ginger ale

Place the water, sugar, cinnamon sticks, and cloves into a saucepan and bring to a gentle boil for 5 minutes. Remove from heat and cool to room temperature.

Strain and discard all spices.

Add pineapple juice and ginger ale just before serving.

Orange Scones with Citrus Butter

⅔ cup flour

2⅔ cups whole wheat flour

¼ cup sugar

2 teaspoons baking soda

2 teaspoons cream of tartar

½ teaspoon salt

½ cup butter

⅓ cup currants or raisins

3 tablespoons grated orange rind

¾ cup buttermilk

⅓ cup molasses

1 egg, slightly beaten

Preheat oven to 375°. Spray two large cookie sheets with nonstick cooking spray.

Mix together the flour, whole wheat flour, sugar, baking soda, cream of tartar, and salt.

Cut in butter with a pastry blender or two butter knives until the mixture is the size of coarse crumbs. Stir in the currants and orange rind.

Add the buttermilk, molasses, and egg. Stir lightly with a fork until a soft dough forms and all dry ingredients are incorporated.

Turn out onto a lightly floured work surface and shape into a ball. Knead dough gently a few times.

Roll the dough out into a ¾ inch thick circle. Cut into diamond shapes using a cookie cutter. Dip the cookie cutter each time into extra flour to prevent sticking.

Continue to cut out scones, until all the dough is used, reworking the scraps.

Bake for 15 minutes or until scones are a light golden brown. Serve warm with Citrus Butter.

Citrus Butter

Makes: ½ cup

1½ tablespoons grated orange rind

½ cup unsalted butter

Combine in a bowl and mix well. Refrigerate two hours before serving.

Turkey Salad and Cranberry Relish Pastry Cups

Makes: 15 servings

Frozen phyllo pastry shells

½ pound roasted turkey

½ cup mayonnaise

Cranberry Relish

Bake the pastry shells as directed on the box. Cool and set aside.

In a food processor blend the turkey and mayonnaise. Add more mayonnaise if needed. Refrigerate until just before serving.

Place a spoonful of the turkey mixture into the pastry shells. Top with cranberry relish. Garnish with edible flowers or parsley.

Cranberry Relish

Makes: 4 cups

9 ounces fresh/frozen cranberries, picked over

1 cup sugar

½ cup water

½ tablespoon grated orange peel

½ cup orange juice

½ cup golden raisins

½ cup finely chopped celery

½ cup chopped walnuts

1 small sweet apple chopped

½ teaspoon ground ginger

In a saucepan heat cranberries, sugar, and water over medium heat until boiling. Stir mixture frequently.

Reduce heat to low and simmer 15 minutes.

Remove from heat and stir in the remaining ingredients.

Cover and refrigerate the relish. The relish may be frozen.

Crab Triangles

Makes: 64 servings

1 pound crabmeat, drained well

⅓–½ cup mayonnaise

¾ cup chopped celery

16 slices of bread (white, whole wheat, or mixed)

Combine the first three ingredients in a bowl and mix well.

Spread the crabmeat mixture evenly over all slices of bread. Cut each slice of bread into four equal triangles. Garnish the open-faced sandwiches with celery leaves or olive slices.

Stuffed Cherry Tomatoes

Makes: 20 servings

20 cherry tomatoes

⅓ cup scallions

½ cup mayonnaise

1 pound bacon, cooked and crumbled

2 tablespoons grated Parmesan cheese

2 tablespoons fresh parsley

Wash and drain cherry tomatoes. Pat dry with a paper towel to remove excess moisture.

Cut a thin slice off the top of each tomato. Scoop out the tomato pulp and discard. Turn the tomatoes over on a paper towel to drain.

Combine all remaining ingredients, mixing well. Fill each tomato and refrigerate several hours.

Pears with Chantilly Dressing

Makes: ¾ cup

Canned pear halves, drained

Chantilly Dressing

½ cup mayonnaise

1 tablespoon orange juice

¼ cup whipped cream

Chopped walnuts, optional

Mix together the mayonnaise and whipped cream.

Add orange juice 1 teaspoon at a time until you reach the flavor you desire.

Place the pears on the serving dish so the scooped-out part faces up.

Place a dollop of dressing in the center of each pear. Garnish with chopped walnuts if desired.

Pineapple Dessert

Makes: 9 servings

¼ cup butter, melted and cooled

1 cup confectioners' sugar

2 tablespoons sugar

1 egg

1 cup graham cracker crumbs

1 cup chilled whipping cream

½ cup butter at room temperature

1 20-oz. can crushed pineapple, drained

Mix crumbs, melted butter, and sugar together. Press ¾ of the mixture firmly into the bottom of an 8-inch cake pan. Refrigerate 5–10 minutes.

In a small bowl beat the remaining butter, confectioners' sugar, and egg until the mixture is light and fluffy. Spread evenly over the crumbs in the cake pan.

In a CHILLED bowl beat whipping cream until stiff; fold in pineapple. Spread over butter mixture. Sprinkle with remaining crumbs around sides.

Chill at least 12 hours. Serve with whipped cream and sliced seasonal fruit as a decoration.

Almond Tea Cake

Makes: 12 servings

1 cup unsalted butter, melted and cooled

6 large eggs, separated

1 cup sugar

½ teaspoon almond extract

¼ cup ground almonds

2½ cups all-purpose flour

2 teaspoons baking powder

½ teaspoon salt

Grated rind of 1 lemon

1 cup milk

Confectioners' sugar

Preheat oven to 350°. Spray bundt pan with nonstick cooking spray and flour pan lightly.

Beat the egg yolks well. Add the sugar, beating well. Add the butter, almond extract, and almonds, mixing well.

Fold in the flour, baking powder, salt, lemon rind, and milk.

Beat the egg whites until stiff, but not dry, and fold in.

Pour batter into the greased bundt pan and bake for 45 minutes or until a toothpick inserted into the middle comes out clean. Cool 10 minutes in the pan, then turn out and let cool completely.

Sprinkle confectioner's sugar on top.

OF COMFORT

As the Dove

As the dove which found no rest
For the sole of her foot, flew back
To the ark her only nest
And found safety there;
Because Noah put forth his hand,
Drew her in from ruin and wrack,
And was more to her than the land
And the air;
So my spirit, like that dove,
Fleeth away to an ark
Where dwelleth a heart of Love,
A hand pierced to save,
Tho' the sun and the moon should fail,
Tho' the stars drop into the dark.

CHRISTINA ROSSETTI

43

Best Friends

*I will comfort you there
as a little one is comforted by its mother.*

Isaiah 66:13, TLB

Tiny snowflakes fling themselves against the living room window. The first snow of the season is usually the quietest and prettiest, but this one came riding in on an unexpected zephyr one Friday afternoon. I start a fire in the cold hearth and put on the kettle. My daughter, Rachel, trudges through the front door.

"How was your day?" I ask my weary-looking fifth-grader.

"Awful."

"What happened?"

"Nothing."

"Do you want to talk about it?"

"No." She drops her backpack on the floor.

"I'm going to have some tea," I tell her. "Would you like to join me?"

"I don't like tea." She plods up the stairs to her room just as the kettle begins to sing.

I was about to dunk a teabag in a mug when my eye catches on Rachel's special teapot in the cupboard. I take it down, rinse it out, and fill it with boiling water and loose tea. The cookies I had set out earlier for Rachel have been ignored, so I take them with me and set up a snowy afternoon tea in front of the fireplace. I light a candle and wait.

I only am three sips into my brew when I hear Rachel's bedroom door open. I don't have to turn around; I can tell by the sound of her steps that her heart is still heavy.

"Who is the other cup for?" she asks.

"You."

"I said I didn't want any tea."

"Okay."

"Why is your tea pink?"

"It's Strawberry Vanilla. I put a little cream in it."

"Oh. May I try a sip?" Rachel samples the drink. At least thirty seconds pass before she says, "Maybe I will have a little."

She takes her time preparing her cup. I watch the snowflakes out the window. Poor little lacy dears, sent spiraling from the heavens without a mother's comforting arm to support them on their way.

Everything within me longs to take my little snowflake princess in my arms and comfort her on her journey through preadolescence. But what do I say? I feel inadequate to the task, and so I wait, slowly sipping my pink tea.

"Mom?" Rachel has drawn her stocking feet under her on the couch. "Is Donna your best friend?"

"Yes, I would say Donna is my best friend."

"How long has Donna been your best friend?"

"Since before you were born."

"Have you and Donna ever had a fight? I've never seen you fight."

"We had a fight on our trip home from England. I didn't like the way she packed the extra suitcase with our souvenirs. I thought the flimsy bag was going to pop open in the belly of the plane."

"Did it?"

"No."

"Then was your fight over?"

"Yes, I suppose it was."

Rachel pours herself some more tea. "Was this teapot in the suitcase you had the fight over?"

"Yes, as a matter of fact, it was."

"It didn't break." Rachel rests it carefully on the table.

"No, I guess it didn't."

"What about your other friends?" she asks. "Have you ever been mad at them?"

"Yes."

"And have they been mad at you?"

"Yes."

"Did you ever not talk to each other for a whole day?"

"Yes. Sometimes longer than a day."

"Why did they get mad at you?"

"Different reasons. One of my friends got mad because I hurt her."

"You hit her?"

"No, I didn't say I hit her. I hurt her. I didn't mean to, but I hurt her on the inside."

"Are you still friends?"

I pause before answering, "Yes. I would say we're still friends. But when you get hurt on the inside it takes longer to heal."

Rachel reaches for a cookie. "If you invited her to your birthday party, do you think she would come?"

"Yes, I think she would."

"What if it was almost her birthday party, and she didn't invite you because she was still mad at you?"

"I would try to talk to her about it and apologize if I hurt her."

"What if you didn't mean to do anything wrong, but your friend said you did, and so you tell her you're sorry, and she says it doesn't matter because she'll never be your friend again?" My little snow princess has melted. A river of tears trickles down her cheeks.

"Then I think all you can do is wait."

"What if you have to wait so long that she has her birthday party without you?"

"Then I guess you would be the one who gets hurt on the inside."

"Where it takes longer to heal," she says.

I wipe her tears with my thumb. "Yes, where it takes longer to heal."

Rachel moves closer. I plant a kiss on each moist cheek.

"Mom, will you wait with me while it heals on my inside?"

"Yes, I will wait with you."

"And Mom? No matter what, will you always be my friend?"

I wrap my willing arms around my only daughter and draw her close so she can hear my heart beating just for her. "Yes, I promise. No matter what, I will always be your friend."

Come little cottage girl, you seem
To want my cup of tea;
And will you take a little cream?
Now tell the truth to me!

BARRY PAIN
"THE POETS AT TEA WORDSWORTH"

Your Kiss

Tiptoeing into my hospital room, you came.
You!
And there you stood beside my bed.

All effort went to sitting
and smiling
and speaking away the pain.

You
Pressed your soft, womanly, motherly, sisterly
Cheek against mine

And kissed
The place beside my ear
Where my hair has gone gray.

You.
No doctor, nor minister, nor spouse
Could have brought with one pure touch
Such comfort as your kiss.

You left,
And in the sterile silence
Lingered the healing beauty of your kiss.

ROBIN JONES GUNN

~Fireside Tea Menu~

Strawberry Vanilla Tea
Shortbread Cookies
Cutout Sandwiches
Choc-O-Nut Pretzels

Shortbread Cookies

Makes: 32 wedges

2 cups unsalted sweet butter

1 cup confectioners' sugar

¼ teaspoon salt

4 cups all-purpose flour

Preheat oven to 375°.

Beat butter until fluffy. Gradually add the sugar and salt. Blend well but do not overwork the dough.

Gradually add the flour.

Turn the dough out onto a work surface that has been sprinkled with a little flour and confectioners' sugar. Separate the dough into two balls.

Pat the balls into two ¾ inch thick circles. Prick several times with a fork and tuck in edges for a smooth look.

Place on baking sheet and refrigerate or freeze for 30 minutes.

Bake for 5 minutes, then reduce the oven to 300° and continue to bake for 45–60 minutes. Shortbread should be golden, not brown. Cut each circle into 16 wedges while still warm.

Cutout Sandwiches

Sandwich bread

Filling

Makes: 1 cup

½ cup cream cheese

1 tablespoon honey

½ cup peanut butter

1 tablespoon orange juice

¼ cup raisins

Blend together cream cheese and peanut butter. Add the raisins, honey, and orange juice. Mix well.

To serve, slightly toast sandwich bread. Using a favorite cookie cutter, cut out shapes in the toasted bread. Spread the cream cheese mixture on the toast. Garnish with more raisins if you desire to make a face or design.

Choc-O-Nut Pretzels

1 package pretzel rods

1 jar chocolate fudge sauce

Chopped nuts, optional

Open the jar of fudge sauce and microwave it until it is a smooth, flowing consistency.

Dip and roll one end of a pretzel in the fudge sauce. Roll the chocolate-covered pretzel in chopped nuts if desired.

Place on waxed paper until set.

OF JOY

My Heart is Like a Singing Bird

My heart is like a singing bird
Whose nest is in a water'd shoot;
My heart is like an apple tree
Whose boughs are bent with thick-set fruit;
My heart is like a rainbow shell
That paddles in a halcyon sea;
My heart is gladder than all these,
Because my love is come to me.

CHRISTINA ROSSETTI

Fluffy Tea in the Tub

The LORD has done great things for us,
and we are filled with joy.

PSALM 126.3, NIV

Once upon our twelve-year anniversary, we made plans. My handsome prince and I were going away for the weekend. Then everything came unhinged, and we had to cancel our plans at the last minute. I knew we would never be able to reschedule. I slipped into the saddest, lowest, bluest of blue moods. By Friday afternoon I had turned into an unbearable ogre.

The neighbor kids were yelling in the backyard so I sent them home. My kids started arguing with each other so I sent them to their rooms. When the clock said 5:40 and my husband wasn't home yet, I sent myself to my room where I flopped on the bed and burrowed into a gigantic mound of warm laundry, fresh from the dryer. I decided I would spend the whole weekend there, buried in the hot, cuddly cotton.

That's when the doorbell rang.

"It's Wendy!" my son announced. "And Dale and Lesley and Katie."

Oh, great! Can't those college kids find some other place to hang out tonight? Maybe if I stop feeding them all the time they'll stop coming.

My children bounced into the bedroom and gleefully announced that Dale and Katie were taking them out for pizza and miniature golf.

Good! They must have looked in the refrigerator and discovered there's no food. I'm too blue to go buy groceries and too low to entertain.

Wendy tapped on the open bedroom door. "Hi. Where's your robe? You have to take your bath."

"Excuse me?"

"We heard your plans fell through. We're going to treat you to a special anniversary dinner. Lesley is cooking. We called Ross. He'll be here in an hour. Come, your tub awaits, your majesty."

"But the laundry…"

"What laundry?" Wendy asked with a magical sweeping motion of her hand. "You have no laundry. You are the queen of anniversary bliss." She draped my robe over her arm and escorted me down the hall.

"But the kids need…"

Wendy waved her hand again. "What kids? You have no children. You are a lady of leisure."

She opened the bathroom door. Soothing classical music circled us. Peach-scented bubble bath gurgled over the tub's rim. A dozen candles flickered like fireflies.

"Now go soak, your highness."

"Go soak my what?"

She shook her head, leaving me alone in the midst of the loveliest pity party anyone had ever thrown for me. Not until I was submerged in the soothing water did I realize this was the first time in the five months we had lived there that I had taken a bubble bath.

A tap, tap sounded at the door, and Wendy entered carrying my silver tea tray. In twelve years of marriage I had never used it. She lowered the tray like a butler and offered me one of my own china teacups peaked with a swirl of whipped cream.

"What is this?"

"Fluffy tea," she said. "I was going to make you some peppermint tea, but then I decided you needed my specialty. A good, strong cup of fluffy tea. Try it."

She left, and I cautiously took a lick. Underneath the whipped cream was more whipped cream. The entire cup was nothing but whipped cream! Fluffy tea!

I didn't expect to laugh aloud, but I did. Seven minutes ago I was blubbering in a nest of T-shirts and little boy boxers. Now, here I was, up to my chin in peachy bubbles, sipping fluffy tea that had come to me on a silver tray in a firefly-lit room where I miraculously had no laundry and no children.

All the gloom scattered. Where did this joy, this sudden, whimsical view of life come from? I was surprised by the rising sense of well-being and delight that filled the air. Joy came soaring in on angels' wings, gracefully gliding over the waves of my disappointment.

For a half-hour I soaked and counted blessings: twelve wonderful years with a loving husband, two healthy children, a cozy home, wondrous friends, and a future brimming with possibilities.

When I returned to my room to dress, I found the laundry folded and put away. A freshly ironed outfit was laid out on the bed for me. A bouquet of daisies brightened up the dresser. The carpet had been vacuumed, and the aroma of lemon chicken filled the house.

I burst out laughing again. Swept away by joy.

"What's so funny?" my husband asked, entering the bedroom.

"This! This Cinderella fairy tale. Did you plan this?"

"No," he said. "Wendy cooked it up. She sent me to tell you that dinner is ready. Wait until you see the dining room. Candles, china, crystal...."

We dined in regal, anniversary bliss. We held hands across the table and said I love you a dozen times. We made plans for what we would do on our next anniversary. And the one after that, and the one after that, and we lived happily ever after. (With the aid of an occasional cup of fluffy tea.)

The cozy fire is bright and gay,
The merry kettle boils away
And hums a cheerful song.
I sing the saucer and the cup;
Pray, Mary, fill the teapot up,
And do not make it strong.

BARRY PAIN "THE POETS AT TEA COWPER"

~Whimsy Tea Menu~

Fluffy Tea
Fancy Store-Bought Cookies (Pepperidge Farm)
Tasty Baked Bananas
Sprinkle Butter Sandwiches

Tasty Baked Bananas

Makes: 2 servings

1 banana

1 tablespoon brown sugar

1 tablespoon flour

¼ teaspoon apple pie spice

½ tablespoon butter

¼ cup chopped pecans, optional

Preheat oven to 450°.

Peel and slice the banana lengthwise and place in a baking dish, tucking slices next to each other.

Mix together remaining ingredients and sprinkle on top of the banana slices.

Cover baking dish with foil and bake for 2–5 minutes. Uncover and broil until topping starts to bubble. Slice in sections and serve.

Sprinkle Butter Sandwiches

Sandwich bread

Butter at room temperature

Cream cheese

Colored sugar

Sprinkles

Using a character cookie cutter, cut out shapes in the sandwich bread.

Spread some slices with butter and sprinkle with colored sugar.

Spread the remaining bread with cream cheese and decorate with colored sprinkles.

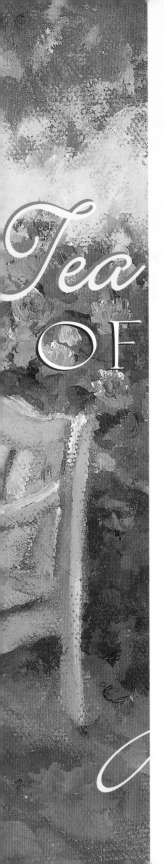

Tea
of Hope

The years teach us much the days never knew.

Dreams in the Moonlight

Last evening I fell asleep in the chair by the window. I was watching the moon rise while sipping chamomile tea from my favorite blue mug. A lovely flood of moonbeams came slipping through the bare arms of the maple tree. The beams fell at my feet and laid for me a shimmering path to the land of dreams. I closed my eyes, and there I was, in that other land, sitting on the tile bathroom counter of the home where I grew up. My dad was watching my mom as she tried to hang new curtains in the small window above the tub.

"Is anyone going to help me with this?" Mom asked.

Instead of answering her, Dad began to tell a story. I sat mesmerized by the sound of his voice, the familiar Irish lilt and rolling inflections. Dad's blue eyes had their twinkle, sparkle, zing once again. As his story unfolded, I felt it go inside me.

"Come on, now," Mom said. "You're going on and on. Let's get this done."

The curtains morphed into the amber-colored beads she really did hang in that bathroom window when I was in eighth grade.

"There's no room for anyone else," Dad tells her.

He slightly raises an eyebrow to me and directs my attention to this determined wife of his. She is balancing on the edge of the bathtub with her arms over her head, fumbling with the tangled beads. All I see from my perch is the broadside of what could only be produced from a gene pool largely made up of thick German potato salad.

I squelch a giggle. Dad's eyes crinkle in the corners.

"And just what do you two think is so funny?" Mom asks without turning around. "Do you think this is easy? I can tell you, it's not. Hanging curtains is nearly impossible to do alone."

I'm the first to sober. Dad isn't of her blood the way I am. I know all about the German potato salad gene pool. I know how to be serious when necessary.

He, however, this undaunted man in my dreams who stands unassisted on two strong legs, continues to give me stories and tickle my imagination with his wit.

Suddenly Mom loses her footing. Before I can go to her, she grabs the windowsill with her fingers. The beaded curtains are gone, and she's waving a card. It's the card they use in their retirement community for residents to post in their front windows in emergencies.

That's when I woke up. Heart pounding, I immediately went for the phone. No one answered my call. On the fourth ring the answering machine picked it up.

"Hello, this is the Joneses."

It's my dad's voice. His voice! That fickle stranger who left him so many years ago is now in my ear, and I'm not dreaming. I drink in the sound as the first syllable lilts higher than the second, like an Irish melody. "Hel-lo, this is the Joneses. We can't come to the phone right now."

The painful truth of his simple sentence chokes me. My dad can't come to the phone right now. Or tomorrow. Or ever. He can't get out of bed. The stroke that overpowered him nearly five years ago left him paralyzed on the right side. It snatched the vision from his right eye and stole his ability to make words. Yet his voice is here. In my ear, in my heart.

"Leave us a message," he says on the machine. "And we'll call you back."

The flat tone sounds, and I try to speak above the thunderous pounding of my heart. "Hi, it's me. Just checking in. I hope everything is okay."

Mom picks up the phone. "Hello?" she asks.

It's always a question when she answers.

I return the question. "Are you okay?"

"Yes. Why?"

"Are you sure? How's Dad? Is everything all right?"

"Yes, of course. Everything is normal."

I know what her "normal" means. It means everything is what it is. Everything is what it has been. It's a long, wobbly line drawn in the desert. A long line drawn by a strong woman who for nearly half a decade has been my father's only full-time nurse. She shaves him, bathes him, and combs his snowy white hair. She reads the mail to him and feeds him through a tube in his stomach. She lifts him into the wheelchair.

This is how she lives out her vow to "love, honor and cherish for better or worse" this man who used to sing with gusto in the shower. A man who drank freely from a fountain of mirth, splashing his charm on any audience that would gather. A man who, with one glance of those silver-blue eyes, spoke into the center of my life. I am also from this whimsical gene pool, and I know I must bend far to once more kiss this Blarney stone. But I must bend.

"I'm coming down the last weekend of this month," I tell Mom.

"Why?" Again with the questions.

"I want to come."

"Good. I ordered new shades for the sunroom. You can help me hang them."

I try hard to remain composed. "Yes, I'll be glad to help you. I imagine it's almost impossible for one person to hang curtains by herself."

A pause, and then she says, "Yes." It's not a question now. "Yes, it is difficult. But it's okay. You can help me." I hear hope in her voice. Hope like a shower of moonbeams breaking through the dark night. Hope like a spring in the desert. Hope comes in through the tiniest opening and breathes its sweetness into the darkest corners. Hope lightens the heaviest of hearts. Hope fills.

So I will go and walk beside my mother for a day as she draws her wobbly line in the sand. I will hold the rod for her.

Then I will sit beside my father, and I will tell him a story with my eyes lit up and twinkling just for him. I will give him the only drink of hope I have to give such a man in such a desert. I will let him hear me giggle one more time.

"Hope" Is a Thing with Feathers

"Hope" is the thing with feathers—
that perches on the soul—
And sings the tune without the words
And never stops—at all—

And sweetest—in the Gale—is heard
And sore must be the storm—

That could abash the little Bird
That kept so many warm—

I've heard it in the chillest land—
And on the strangest Sea—
Yet, never, in Extremity,
It asked a crumb—of Me.

EMILY DICKINSON

Now Came Still Evening On

The starry host rode brightest, till the moon
Rising in clouded majesty, at length,
Apparent queen, unveiled her peerless light,
And o'er the dark her silver mantle threw.

JOHN MILTON

~Moonlight Tea Menu~

English Breakfast Tea
Graham Bread with Currant Jelly
Harvest Moon Apples
Sliced Cheddar Cheese

Graham Bread

Makes: 2 loaves

4 cups graham flour or whole wheat flour

½ cup nonfat dry milk

1 tablespoon salt

2 packages dry yeast

3 cups water

½ cup molasses

2 tablespoons butter

4–4½ cups unbleached white flour

Preheat oven to 350°. Grease two 9x5 inch bread pans.

Combine in bowl 3 cups graham flour, dry milk powder, salt, and yeast.

Heat water, molasses, and butter in a saucepan until butter is melted. Pour liquid over the flour mixture. Beat mixture with an electric mixer for 3 minutes.

Stir in 1 additional cup of graham flour and gradually the white flour; knead 5 minutes using additional white flour if necessary.

Place in a greased bowl, turn and let rise until double. Punch down, divide dough in half, and shape into loaves. Place in greased bread pans. Cover and let rise 40–45 minutes.

Bake for 40–45 minutes. Test for doneness when bread sounds hollow when you tap on the top.

Serve with currant jelly.

Harvest Moon Apples

Makes: 8 servings

8 medium cooking apples, cored

¾ cup raisins

⅓ cup plus 2 tablespoons brown sugar

¾ teaspoon ground cinnamon

¼ cup unbleached flour

¼ cup butter at room temperature

⅓ cup finely chopped walnuts, or other nuts

¾ cup orange juice

¾ cup water

Preheat oven to 375°. Grease a 13 x 9 inch baking dish.

Stuff each apple equally with raisins. Set aside.

Combine sugar, cinnamon, and flour in a separate mixing bowl. Stir well. Cut in butter using a pastry blender until the mixture resembles coarse meal. Stir in walnuts with a fork.

Stuff the flour mixture equally in the center of each apple. Pour orange juice and water in the bottom of the baking dish.

Bake for 1 hour or until the apples are tender when tested with a fork. Baste apples often with the juices in the pan.

Serve immediately. Garnish with whipped topping or ice cream.

Garden Tea
OF PEACE

Night Among the English Lakes

Raised are the dripping oars—
Silent the boat: the lake,
Lovely and soft as a dream,
Swims in the sheen of the moon.

MATTHEW ARNOLD

Great Lady's Hands

A heart at peace gives life to the body....

PROVERBS 14:30, NIV

I wish you could see my grandmother's hands. Ever since I was a child I thought her hands were extraordinary. She keeps her nails short, files them herself, and paints them with two coats of sheer gloss. Her palms are worn, etched with a hundred fascinating lines. Along the top of her hands run pale, purple veins—superhighways of the strength that flows through her. She's been a widow for twenty years and lives by herself.

My grandma is ninety-three years old.

And she has hands as soft as rose petals in springtime.

Last month I visited Great Lady, as we all call her. She recently had been given some blackberry tea in a fancy tin and invited me to share a cup with her. With slow movements and cheery conversation, Great Lady prepared a little plate of cheese and crackers to accompany our tea.

I sat beside her at the kitchen table and watched as Great Lady's gentle hands folded and her head bowed. I did the same. We prayed the simple mealtime prayer I have heard her pray since my earliest memory. "Come, Lord Jesus, be our guest, and let these gifts to us be blessed. Amen."

Her hands reached for the plate of crackers, and she politely offered them first to me. There actually was only room on the table for our teacups and the plate of crackers. The rest of the table was stacked with an intricate display of whatnot. Great Lady called it her "table garden."

On my right were magazines and catalogs. In front of me waited a stack of photos, all labeled and sorted. Next to the photos was a small dish with tiny seashells and a cross necklace on a long silver chain. A jarful of jelly beans rested on top of a pair of slippers, which sat atop a notebook. Beside Great Lady was a journal with a pen, a dozen postcards, and the flip calendar I gave her for Christmas with a Scripture for each day.

As we began our afternoon tea at her table garden, her hand reached for the photos first. Did I know that Casey's youngest was starting kindergarten in the fall? No, I didn't realize that. Had I seen any of the pictures from Tom and Sue's trip to the Korean War Memorial in D.C.? Emily is playing softball again this year. Doesn't Jessie look cute with her new short hair? Did I know that Chuck named his dog "Oreo"?

I nodded and gave the appropriate "Oh?" and "Hmmm" as each photo was viewed.

She presented me with the dish of seashells. "I collected these early one morning on the beach at Waikiki. It must have been more than thirty years ago. I thought you might like them. And, oh, say, could you use a pair of nice slippers? These were given to me, but I already have a perfectly good pair. You can use them, can't you?"

Her hands moved on to the catalog where she showed me a picture of a bedspread with sweet purple violets. "I was thinking of getting this bedspread. What do you think?"

"I think it's perfect. As a matter of fact, I'd like to get it for you as an early birthday present." I pulled my credit card from my purse as Great Lady protested. I dialed the 800 number and placed the order. She shook her head at the marvels of this modern world. In a few days her new bedspread would appear on her doorstep, and she didn't have to write a check or fill out a form or find someone to take her to the post office. Amazing.

We went through the postcards, sampled the jelly beans, discussed a clipping from the newspaper, and moved on to the notebook. Great Lady opened to where she had been recording her memoirs.

I smiled broadly as I realized what this teatime was all about. She needed me to sit with her while she weeded this indoor garden of her life. A garden in miniature, collected there at her kitchen table. Her grandchildren were her flowers. The great-grandchildren her wildflowers. She wanted some company while she tidied up.

That task accomplished, she then invited me into a deeper, hidden garden, the garden of her heart, as she shyly asked, "Would you like to hear a poem I wrote?"

As soon as she read the last line, I told her I loved it. She promised to write out a copy for me. I pictured those beautiful hands of hers, on some rainy afternoon, slowly printing each letter. It would take her half a day, and I would treasure it always.

She told me about cutting her hair into a Roaring Twenties bob when she was in high school. She was the first girl in her small town to do so. None of her ten brothers or sisters knew she was going to do it, and, oh, how her father's face turned red! He was the local Lutheran minister, you know.

I listened with delight, honored to be invited into the hidden garden. I couldn't take my eyes off her hands. Her beautiful hands. Hands that have lived nearly a century. I knew that not all of those years were softened by strolls on the beach at sunrise. She had worked hard and long to properly tend this garden of her life.

And now I saw the fruit of her life's labor. I could see it in her hands. They were peaceful hands. Soft, smooth hands that did not tremble or dart about nervously. They glided about this table garden of hers like two swans on a lake. Only a heart at peace could fold two such hands and daily invite the Lord Jesus to come be her guest.

I left Great Lady's cottage that afternoon with six blackberry tea bags, a pair of slippers, a dish of tiny shells from Waikiki, and the settled assurance that in the hidden garden of my heart, I, too, could know a lifetime of peace. It would start with an invitation from my lips that begins, "Come, Lord Jesus."

A Day of Sunshine

O gift of God! O perfect day,
Whereon shall no man work, but play;
Whereon it is enough for me,
Not to be doing, but to be!

HENRY WADSWORTH LONGFELLOW

~Hidden Garden Tea Menu~

Blackberry Tea
Assorted Cheeses
Savory Crackers
Apple Nut Tea Bread

Apple Nut Tea Bread

Makes: 2 loaves

1 cup milk

1 tablespoon white vinegar

1 teaspoon vanilla

1½ cups brown sugar

⅔ cup vegetable oil

1 egg

1 teaspoon baking soda

1 teaspoon salt

1 teaspoon cinnamon

2 cups all-purpose flour

½ cup whole wheat flour

1½ cups diced apples

⅓ cup chopped walnuts

Topping

½ cup sugar

½ cup melted butter

Preheat oven to 325°. Grease and flour two 8½ x 4½ inch loaf pans.

Combine the milk and white vinegar and set aside.

In a large bowl mix together the brown sugar, vegetable oil, egg, milk mixture, and vanilla.

In a separate bowl combine the baking soda, salt, cinnamon, all-purpose flour, and whole wheat flour. Add the flour mixture to the milk mixture. Fold in the diced apples and walnuts.

Pour the mixture equally into the two loaf pans.

Combine the topping ingredients. Sprinkle the top of each loaf with the sugar topping.

Bake for 60 minutes.

Popular Types of Tea

Perhaps you already knew that all three types of tea—black, oolong, and green—come from the same plant, *Camellia sinensis*, a bushy member of the evergreen family. But did you know that from these three types come more than three thousand varieties?

Some teatime choices include:

English Breakfast

The most popular of all teas, English Breakfast was developed more than a hundred years ago by the Scottish Tea Master Drysdale in Edinburgh. Marketed at first as "Breakfast Tea," it became popular in England due to the craze Queen Victoria created for all things Scottish. (The summer home of Victoria and Albert was the Highland castle of Balmoral.) Teashops in London, however, changed the name to "English Breakfast Tea." A blend of fine black teas, often including some Keemun (grown in northeastern China), it should be offered with milk or lemon.

Irish Breakfast

The Irish say that a proper cup of tea should be "strong enough for a mouse to trot on." Irish Breakfast is, therefore, a full-flavored, dark tea blended from Assam (tea grown in northeastern India). Because of its rich taste, Irish Breakfast is served with lots of sugar and milk.

Many people consider cream too heavy for tea and prefer milk served at room temperature, never cold, as it cools the tea too quickly.

Prince of Wales

This common teatime brew blends fine Chinese teas into a lush, deep, dark color. Milk and sugar make excellent companions for this cheering cup.

Caravan

A blended tea created in imperial Russia, from teas brought overland by camel from Asia. Since the trade routes were dangerous and supplies unsteady, Russian tea merchants combined varying incoming tea cargoes, creating a mix of Chinese and Indian black teas. Caravan is generally served with honey and lemon slices studded with cloves.

Earl Grey

While Earl Grey (1764-1845) was the prime minister of England under William IV, tea legends have it that the blend was given to him by a Chinese mandarin seeking to influence trade relations. This smoky tea blends Darjeeling, black tea, and the oil of bergamot (an Italian citrus fruit). Fragrant in aroma and taste, Earl Grey often is drunk without any milk, sugar, or lemon.

One should never serve lemon to a guest if she requests milk. The lemon would curdle the milk.

Polly put the kettle on, we'll all have tea.

TRADITIONAL SONG

Darjeeling

Grown in the Darjeeling mountainous area of India, this tea offers a fragrant, full-bodied scent but a light flavor. Often served in the afternoon, guests traditionally drink it plain. A little lemon might be added, but not milk since milk would mask the qualities that make the tea unique.

Oolong

This elegant tea produces a clear, fragrant brew. Originally grown in the Fukien province of China, Oolong was imported to England in 1869. A cross between green and black teas, it is fermented to achieve a delicious, fruity taste that makes milk, lemon, and sugar unthinkable. With such clarity, it is perfect for afternoon use with such tea fare as cucumber sandwiches.

Keemun

The most famous of China's black teas, this mellow tea can be drunk unadorned or with sugar or milk. Lemon should not be offered, as the combined tastes are too tart.

Ceylon

Grown in the soaring altitudes of Sri Lanka, this tea produces a rich, golden brew. Often used in blends, it also works nicely on its own.

Green

Green tea comprises only ten percent of the world's produced tea. The Japanese tea service in which green tea is used is an art form in and of itself. Green tea generally isn't part of the Western afternoon tea tradition.

Historic Day for Tea

In the summer of 1904, exhibitors from around the world gathered at America's first World's Fair in St. Louis. One of the merchants, Richard Blechynden, was a tea plantation owner. He planned to give away free samples of hot tea to fair visitors. But when a heat wave hit, no one was interested. To save his investment of time and travel, he dumped a load of ice into the brewed tea and served the first "iced tea." The beverage (along with the Egyptian fan dancer) was the hit of the Fair.

— Calm After the Storm —

How calm, how beautiful comes on
The stilly hour, when storms are gone:
When warring winds have died away,
And clouds, beneath the glancing ray,
Melt off, and leave the land and sea
Sleeping in bright tranquillity.

THOMAS MOORE